The Hidden Ireland

Accom
Histori

2001

Colour Reproduction & Printed by W&G Baird

Published by Hidden Ireland Heritage Holidays Limited
P.O. Box 31, Westport, Co. Mayo

The front cover photograph and that of house number 24 are reproduced by kind permission of the Country Life Picture Library.

The Hidden Ireland

The Hidden Ireland is a unique collection of private houses offering visitors the opportunity to sample Irish country life at its very best, in a style not usually experienced by the ordinary tourist. Our houses are not hotels, guesthouses or B&B's but historic listed buildings of great character, with unusual and interesting owners who enjoy sharing their homes with appreciative visitors.

Do not expect a reception desk, bar or residents' lounge. Instead, you will find a warm welcome and a refreshing drink in a comfortable drawing room filled with family heirlooms.

Our members own a number of Ireland's Great Country Houses, once the centres of large estates. These were designed by famous architects and were lived-in and visited by famous figures of former times. Other houses are smaller, but no less beautiful or interesting. Many are surrounded by landscaped parks or gardens and have belonged to the family for generations.

Recently we have added a selection of Town houses, all carefully chosen to offer traditional Hidden Ireland standards in an urban setting. Town Houses are not required to serve dinner (though several do) and are indistinguishable from their rural counterparts in all other ways.

You will meet the owners, always a fund of local information and knowledge. Their houses reflect their hobbies and interests and they will be happy to share them with you. Some are particularly keen on wine, painting, gardening, music or literature, while others are devotees of country sport, horses, golf or other outdoor pursuits. Whatever your interests, your hosts will do their best to ensure that your stay is as enjoyable as possible.

One night does not usually give you enough time to see the house and grounds, visit neighbouring attractions and get to know your hosts, so we strongly urge you to consider staying at least two nights in each house. Visitors who arrive late and leave directly after breakfast will miss the essence of The Hidden Ireland – the experience of becoming a pampered private guest in the relaxed and intimate atmosphere of an Historic Irish Country House.

We provide a real and interesting alternative to conventional accommodation. There are activities for everyone, including access to the best hunting, shooting and fishing in the country, but our houses are also ideal if you need a restful break. We know you will enjoy the country house-party atmosphere of another era, in splendid surroundings, with good food and wine, and an air of exclusivity, privacy and calm.

Peter Mantle, Chairman

SEE IRELAND FROM A DIFFERENT PERSPECTIVE

THE IRISH LANDMARK TRUST

...From elegant Georgian Dublin to the shores of Donegal,
From a tiny gothic Gatelodge to a striking medieval Castle,
From the wildness of a lighthouse to the tranquillity of a woodland Cottage.

...And from this summer, experience the life of a lighthouse keeper in Cork or Antrim and explore hidden Waterford. All our properties are of historic and architectural merit, and provide a unique and exciting way to see Ireland.

For a brochure on all properties available for holiday rental. please contact The Irish Landmark Trust, Tel: +353 1 670 4733 Fax: + 353 1 670 4887 E-mail: landmark@iol.ie

General Information

Country Houses are labelled   **C**

Townhouses are labelled   **T**

Reservations – Our houses are private family homes so it is wise (and often essential) to book in advance. **Please make your reservation by contacting the house directly by phone, fax or e-mail.**

Cancellation and No-shows – Each house operates its own cancellations policy (with varying terms) and a charge is usually made whenever a cancellation occurs. If this takes place at the last moment, or if you fail to arrive, you will probably have to pay in full (including the price of dinner, if booked). Please enquire when making your reservation.

Arrival Time – We suggest you arrive in the late afternoon – not before 4.30 p.m. This will give you time to settle in and relax before dinner. If you wish to arrive earlier please contact your hosts in advance: otherwise there may be nobody to greet you.

Visitors arriving on Trans-Atlantic Flights – If your flight arrives early in the morning, please remember that your room is unlikely to be available until much later in the day. **If you wish to ensure that your room is ready on arrival you should make your reservation for the preceding night.**

Prices – Rates shown are per person, per night, and are based on two persons sharing a double room. Most houses charge a supplement for single occupancy and this is clearly indicated. The price always includes a full, traditional Irish breakfast.

More expensive houses may have a higher standard of grandeur and luxury while less expensive houses are usually simpler, though no less comfortable or interesting. All houses are of a high standard, with friendly owners, and all give good value for money.

Credit Cards – All our houses welcome credit cards; the cards accepted are clearly identified under individual entries.

The Euro – Euro notes and coins are not yet in circulation but conversions are made automatically for visitors who wish to pay by credit card. Otherwise accounts are payable in Irish pounds. **This does not apply to houses in Northern Ireland, which are in the sterling area.**

Special Rates – Many houses have special rates for long stays, groups or family parties, particularly at mid-week or in the quiet season. Our houses are particularly attractive when taken-over by a single party. Please check rates with individual houses.

Tipping – We are all private houses and do not have a set service charge but it is customary to leave a small gratuity for the staff. Naturally this is at your discretion, and is always much appreciated.

Bathrooms – The majority of our houses have private en-suite bathrooms. Some bathrooms may be across the corridor, though still exclusive to the bedroom, in order to preserve the architectual integrity of the house. In a very small number of cases bathrooms may be shared and, if so, this is indicated under the entry for your house. If a private en-suite bathroom is important to you, we advise you to check when booking.

Children – Many houses welcome small children: others do not. Usually, this is due to valuable antique furnishings or natural hazards, such as fast-flowing rivers. Some houses do not permit very small children in the dining room at night (in consideration of other guests) while others offer special meals and rates for small children. This is usually indicated very clearly but please check the situation when making your reservation.

Dinner – All our country houses (and a number of our town houses) serve dinner at night but, in a number of instances, this is only available for five nights per week. You should check if dinner is available while making your reservation and, if it is not, there is usually a choice of good restaurants within easy reach. It is usually necessary to book dinner well in advance of arrival and your hosts will need to know if you intend to dine in each evening, or not, at an early date.

You may find yourself dining by candlelight, frequently sitting with your hosts and their other guests (unless they are cooking your meal). Most houses seat the guests at one large table, which stimulates conversation, while others have smaller, separate tables. Guests all dine at the same time, usually 7.30 or 8.00 p.m.

General Information (cont.)

Naturally, all meals are served using the finest regional produce, often from the host's own farm or garden, cooked to perfection. Most houses offer a table d'hôte menu, usually of four or five courses with no choice, so we advise you to check when making your reservation and to give advance warning of any dietary requirements or allergies.

Wine - Most houses have a wine licence (and several have excellent cellars). Houses without a wine licence are clearly indicated, Guests in these houses are normally welcome to bring their own wine.

Foreign Languages - Most hosts have a good or fluent knowledge of a European language. Please enquire when making your reservation.

The Hidden Ireland
P.O. Box 31, Westport, Co. Mayo

Tel: + 353-1-662-7166
Fax: + 353-1-662-7144
USA toll free: 1-800-688-0299
email: info@hidden-ireland.com
www.hidden-ireland.com

Annesbrook

C

Annesbrook is an 18th century country house set in ten acres of gardens and woodland in the Boyne Valley, 35km from Dublin. The house is close to the archaeological sites at Newgrange and Monasterboice as well as many other ancient monuments. Also nearby are the beautiful Butterstream and Malahide gardens, Baltray and Portmarnock golf courses, a cross country riding facility and an indoor equestrian centre.

Interesting architectural features at Annesbrook include the portico and gothic dining room, both built on for a visit by George IV. Another distinguished visitor was Thackeray. The formal hospitality of those days has been replaced by a relaxed family atmosphere. The walled garden and orchard still provide most of the produce for the house, which has an air of great tranquillity.

* Five rooms, all with private bathrooms
* B&B: £30–£40 (€38.10–€50.80)
  Single supplement: £10 (€12.70)
* Dinner: £23 (€29.21) 7pm, 24 hrs notice, unavailable
  Tuesday & Wednesday
* No pets please
* Open April 15 to September 30
* Advance booking essential
* Groups of 6+ possible in winter
* Credit Cards: Visa, Mastercard

Kate Sweetman
Annesbrook,
Duleek, Co. Meath.

Directions:
1km south of Duleek
on R152.

Tel: +353 41 9823293 Fax: +353 41 9823024
Guest Tel: +353 41 9880976

email:sweetman@annesbrook.com
www.annesbrook.com

Map Ref.

1

Ardnamona

Ardnamona, on Lough Eske under the Blue Stack mountains is described in the Topographical Dictionary of Ireland 1837, as "one of the most picturesque domains in rural Ireland". The writer Violet French was captivated: "I first saw Ardnamona from the lake on a fine August evening, romantic and picturesque with an appealing beauty which clings around the heart as if it belonged to a dream world".

Ardnamona has glorious gardens, planted by Sir Arthur Wallace in the 1880s. Many of the seeds and cuttings came from the Imperial Gardens at Peking and the palace gardens in Kathmandu. It is designated a National Heritage Garden and has been described as "wild gardening at its most exuberant and refined; a Himalayan mountain slope cloaked with a primeval rhododendron forest, 60 feet tall, with a carpet of leaves underfoot".

* Six bedrooms, all with private bathrooms
* B&B: £45–£55 (€57.15–€69.85)
  Single supplement: £10 (€12.70)
* Dinner: £25 (€31.75) 8.30pm. 24 hours notice, unavailable Sunday
* Special interest and group bookings welcome all year round
* Children welcome. Dogs allowed outside
* Closed 20th December until 2nd January
* Advance booking essential
* Russian and French spoken
* Credit Cards: Amex, Visa, Mastercard

Kieran and Amabel Clarke
Ardnamona,
Lough Eske, Co. Donegal.

Tel: +353 73 22650 Fax: +353 73 22819

email:mail@ardnamona.com
www.ardnamona.com

Directions:
From Donegal Town take N15 towards Letterkenny. After 5km take small turning on left marked Harveys Point and Lough Eske. Go straight for 7 kms. Look for gate lodge and white gates on right.

Map Ref.
2

Assolas

Assolas is a charming 17th century house, set among ancient trees, with lawns sweeping down to the river. The Bourke family has lived here for generations and has welcomed guests to their house for more than thirty years.

The gardens – winner of the coveted National Garden Award – produce fruit, vegetables and herbs, which are the foundation of Hazel's famous regional food, while the atmosphere is enhanced by a well-deserved reputation for hospitality and fine food, complimented by an excellent wine list.

Assolas is within an hour's drive of all the Southwest's premier attractions, such as Blarney Castle, Dingle, The Ring of Kerry and the cities of Cork and Kinsale. Visitors can enjoy lawn tennis, boating, croquet, salmon or trout fishing (and coarse fishing). There are numerous golf courses nearby (golf at Kanturk is complimentary) while, for hill-walkers, the region abounds with walks of varying grades and distances.

Private groups are welcome at any time of the year – by prior arrangement.

* Six double/Twin rooms (3 superior) all with private bathroom
* B&B £60–£85 (€76.20–€107.95)
* Single supplement £10 (€12.70)
* Dinner £30 (€38.10) 7–8pm, book by noon
* Credit Cards: Visa, Mastercard
* Open 15 March until 5 November
* Children welcome/Separate high tea

Joe & Hazel Bourke
Assolas Country House,
Kanturk, Co. Cork.

Tel: +353 29 50015
Fax: +353 29 50795

email:assolas@eircom.net
www.assolas.com

Directions:
Signposts from the N72 (Mallow–Killarney Road) 8 miles west of Mallow. Assolas is 3½ miles Northeast of Kanturk.

Map Ref.
3

Ballinkeele House

Ballinkeele, built in 1840, is the ancestral home of the Maher family. The house is set in 350 acres of game-filled parkland, with fine stands of mature trees, several lakes and ponds and an atmosphere of complete tranquility.

With its distinguished classical portico, Ballinkeele provides a civilised base for a relaxing break in a comfortable, lived-in family home, beautifully maintained by John and Margaret, the present owners. The walls are covered with portraits and prints and the furniture is original to the house while bedrooms offer the ideal combination of space, comfort and character. Margaret is a member of Euro Toques and uses fresh local ingredients, including produce from farm and garden, to great effect.

Ballinkeele is an excellent base for touring the Southeast. There are bicycles and wellingtons to explore the surroundings or you can enjoy a game of croquet on the lawn. Amenities include the long sandy beach at Curracloe (the Normandy Beaches in Saving Private Ryan) with 6 golf courses, fishing and riding available nearby. The highlight of the year is the world-famous Wexford Opera Festival, held each October.

* Five rooms, all with private bathrooms
* Smoking is not permitted in bedrooms
* B&B: £45–£60 (€57.15–€76.20)
  Single supplement: £12 (€15.24)
* Dinner: £26 (€33.02) 7.30pm, please book by noon, unavailable Monday
* No dogs please
* Open March 1 to November 12
* Groups by arrangement
* Credit Cards: Amex, Visa, Mastercard

John and Margaret Maher
Ballinkeele House,
Ballymurn,
Enniscorthy, Co.Wexford.

Tel: +353 53 38105 Fax: +353 53 38468

email: info@ballinkeele.com
www.ballinkeele.com

Directions:
From Wexford take N11 north to Oilgate village and turn right at signpost. From Enniscorthy, take N11 south to Oilgate village and turn left at signpost.

Map Ref.
4

Ballyowen is an unaltered classical Georgian house, dating from the middle of the eighteenth century and set in a heavily wooded park on the slopes of Mount O'Meara, five miles north of the historic town of Cashel.

Six generations of the McCan family have lived and farmed at Ballyowen. Frank, the present owner and his wife, Marie, opened the house to guests more than ten years ago, and have recently been joined by their son, Colm, and his wife Aoife (who both trained at the famous Ballymaloe House and Cookery School).

Aoife's menus change daily and rely on the farm's own produce, prepared with imagination and flair. Bedrooms are large and comfortable, with views over the park with its specimen trees. This is an ideal centre for golf, fishing, horse racing, trekking and visiting historic sites, or for those who prefer to sit back and enjoy a relaxing break.

---

* 3 bedrooms, 2 en-suite
* Price per person sharing £40 (€50.80)
  Single supplement: £7 (€8.89)
* Dinner: £22 (€27.94). Book by noon
* Special rates for longer stays. Bedrooms are non-smoking
* Open mid-February to mid-November
* Not recommended for very young children
* Dogs by arrangement
* Credit Cards: Visa, Mastercard and Amex

Frank and Marie McCan
Ballyowen House,
Cashel, Co. Tipperary.

Tel: +353 62 61265

email: info@ballyowenhouse.com
www.ballyowenhouse.com

Directions:
Turn right off the N8 four miles north of Cashel (signposted Dualla). Gates on the right after one mile.

Ballyvolane House

Originally built in 1728, Ballyvolane was remodelled 120 years later in Italianate style. Surrounded by woodlands, with formal terraced gardens and recently restored trout lakes, the house has a charming, peaceful atmosphere. A fine pillared hall features a Bluthner baby grand piano.

Ballyvolane has private salmon fishing on 13 km of the renowned River Blackwater, with a wide variety of spring and summer beats. The beautiful Blackwater Valley, with its many gardens and historic sites, is well worth touring. The heritage town of Lismore, Blarney and Bunratty Castles, the Rock of Cashel, the Ring of Kerry, Fota Wildlife Park and Waterford Crystal can all be visited easily from Ballyvolane. Sea fishing, beaches, riding, tennis, hill-walking and 16 golf courses are all within a 45 km drive.

* Six double rooms, all with private bathrooms
* B&B: £40–£50 (€50.80–€63.50)
  Single supplement: £15 (€19.05)
* Dinner: £26 (€33.02) (8pm, 10 hours notice)
* Open 1 January to 22 December
* Children accepted.
* No dogs in house
* Credit Cards: Amex, Visa, Mastercard

Jeremy and Merrie Green
Ballyvolane House,
Castlelyons, Co. Cork.

Tel: +353 25 36349
Fax: +353 25 36781

email:ballyvol@iol.ie
www.ballyvolanehouse.ie

Directions:
From Cork, turn right off N8 at the River Bride, just before Rathcormac. Follow signs for house.

Map Ref.
6

Bantry House

Bantry House has belonged to the White family since 1739. It is one of the finest stately mansions in Ireland, furnished with a wonderful collection of furniture and works of art gathered by the 2nd Earl of Bantry during his European travels. He also designed the grounds with a formal Italian garden and a 'staircase to the sky' behind the house, overlooking the sea. Bantry House has been open to the public since 1946.

There is a private dining room, sitting room and billiard room for guests. Within the area are plenty of sporting facilities. Bantry is an excellent base from which to tour the famous sites and scenery of West Cork and Kerry.

Egerton is a keen trombone player so there is always music at Bantry, with frequent concerts in the library.

---

* 8 rooms en-suite
* B&B: March and October £75.00 (€95.25)
  April–September £85.00 (€107.95)
  Single supplement £10.00 (€12.70)
* Dinner: £25 (€31.75) 8 hours notice, ask about availability when booking
* Children (under 10) free in parents room, otherwise please enquire for rates
* No pets in rooms
* Credit Cards: Amex, Visa, Mastercard

Mr. & Mrs. Egerton Shelswell White
Bantry House,
Bantry, Co. Cork.

Tel: +353 27 50047
Fax: +353 27 50795

Directions:
Main entrance in
Bantry town.

www.hidden-ireland.com/bantry

Blanchville House

Surrounded by rich farmland just outside the mediaeval city of Kilkenny, this is an ideal place to relax and get away from it all. The house was built in 1800 and has been lovingly restored by the Phelan family, retaining many original features and furnishings. Guests at Blanchville are assured of good food and a very warm welcome.

Our hard tennis court and billiard and games rooms are available for guests. There are several golf courses within 30 minutes drive, including the Championship course at Mount Juliet, while riding, shooting, fishing and flying are all available locally.

If you are interested in high-quality, handmade Irish crafts, Blanchville is at the centre of 'The Kilkenny Craft trail', or you can use us as a base for exploring the Southeast's numerous historical and archaeological sites.

---

* Six rooms, all with private bathrooms
* B&B: £35–£37.50 (€44.45–€47.62).
  Single supplement: £8 (€10.16)
* Dinner: £25 (€31.75) 24 hours notice, unavailable Sunday and Monday
* No children under 10
* Dogs by arrangement
* Self-catering coachhouses available
* Open March 1 to November 1
* Credit Cards: Amex, Visa, Mastercard.

Tim & Monica Phelan
Blanchville House,
Dunbell, Maddoxtown,
Co. Kilkenny.

Tel: +353 56 27197
Fax: +353 56 27636

email:info@blanchville.ie
www.blanchville.ie

Directions:
Take N10
Carlow/Dublin road
from Kilkenny. First
right 1km after the
Pike Pub (signposted).
Left at next
crossroads, entrance
2km on left.

Map Ref.
8

Boltown House

Built in the mid 18th century, Boltown House is set in 200 acres of rolling farmland and prime grazing which has produced many winning race horses over the years. With pleasant gardens and a charming atmosphere, the house offers a peaceful refuge just an hour's drive from Dublin.

Susan is an especially good cook, drawing herbs and other produce from Boltown's kitchen garden. There are many archaeological sites nearby, including Trim and Newgrange, and guests may also visit the wonderful gardens at Butterstream, Ballinlough Castle and The Grove or play golf on a number of different courses in the area.

* Three double bedrooms, all with private bathroom
* B&B: £35 (€44.45). Single supplement: £10 (€12.70)
* Dinner: £24 (€30.80) 8pm, or by special arrangement, 12 hours notice
* Children and well-behaved dogs welcome
* Open 10 January to 20 December
* Advance booking essential
* Credit Cards: Amex, Visa, Mastercard

Jean & Susan Wilson
Boltown House,
Kells,
Co Meath.

Tel: +353 46 43605
Fax: +353 46 43036

email:boltown@iolfree.ie
www.hidden-ireland.com/boltown

Directions:
From Kells take Oldcastle/Castlepollard road for 4 miles, take second left (Kilskyre) after petrol station. House 3/4 mile on right.

Map Ref.
9

Castle ffrench was built in 1779 by Sir Charles ffrench, Mayor of Galway. Set in rolling parkland this listed Georgian house with its elaborate plasterwork has a warm peaceful atmosphere. Blazing log fires, comfortable rooms, good food and wine make Castle ffrench the perfect escape from the stresses of the 20th century.

Hunting is available with five registered packs of hounds. Golf and fishing are also available locally. Nature walks with picnic lunches are also organised through the peat bogs or the less energetic might prefer to paint or bird watch. Bill is a keen carriage driver and breeds Arab horses while Sheila is an enthusiastic horse-woman and artist. Castle ffrench is a no smoking house.

* Four bedrooms with private bathrooms
* B&B: £75 (€95.25). Price per room £150 (€190.50)
* Dinner: £35 (€44.45) 24 hours notice, unavailable Sunday and Monday
* Open 20 April until 31 October. Otherwise by arrangement
* Minimum stay at weekends (2 nights)
* Unsuitable for children under 10 years
* Kennels available
* Credit cards: Visa, Mastercard

Bill and Sheila Bagliani
Castle ffrench, Ballinamore Bridge,
Co. Galway.

Tel: 0903 22288
Fax: 0903 22003

email:castleffrench@eircom.net
www.castleffrench.com

Directions:
From Ballinasloe head for Ahascragh. Go through town for 1 mile, at school turn right, signed for Ballygar. 3 miles to our gates on right side. House 1 mile up drive. From Athlone take Tuam road and turn off towards Mt. Bellew. Look for sign to house.

Map Ref.
10

Clifden House

Clifden is a listed, early Georgian house hiding on the wooded shore of Lake Inchiquin, the southern boundary of the remarkable Burren region. Abandoned for many years, the house is slowly being coaxed into compromise with the twentieth century. The resulting mixture of gentle ruin and epicurean comfort somehow sidesteps time.

Bernadette is passionate about cooking and her organic fruits, vegetables and meats come from the garden and the nearby family farm. The River Fergus flows through the stableyard and, along with a host of lakes, provides trout and pike fishing. Shooting, riding, hunting, golf, walking and the great wealth of natural history of the Burren are all on the doorstep. Shannon Airport is just 20 miles away.

* Four bedrooms, all with private bathrooms
* B&B: £38 (€48.26)
* Dinner £25 (€31.75) 8pm, book by 11am
* No wine licence (guests may bring their own)
* Children welcome
* Open mid-March–early-November
* Groups welcome at other times
* Credit cards: Amex, Visa, Mastercard

Bernadette & Jim Robson
Clifden House,
Corofin,
Co Clare.

Tel & fax: +353 65 6837692

email:clifdenhousecountyclare@eircom.net
www.clifdenhouse-countyclare.com

Directions:
In Corofin (8 miles north of Ennis) turn west at northern end of village, then take 2nd minor road on right. Signposted 200 yds later on right.

Map Ref.
11

Clonalis House C

Clonalis House is the ancestral home of the O'Conors of Connacht, descendants of Ireland's last High Kings and traditional Kings of Connacht. Built on a wooded 700 acre estate, Clonalis is a comfortable 45 roomed Victorian Italianate mansion. The house offers our guests an opportunity to explore the rich history of the O'Conors by browsing through our archive and library dating from the 16th Century and examining such heirlooms as Carolan's Harp and the O'Conor Coronation Stone.

Confident of a warm welcome and the enjoyment of good food, guests can retire to one of our four poster or half tester beds. Clonalis is a ideal location from which to explore Galway City, Sligo and Mayo, all of which are within one hour's drive.

* Three double rooms and one twin room all with bath
* B&B: £48–£52 (€60.96–€66.04).
  Single supplement: £8 (€10.16)
* Reduction for three or more nights
* Dinner: £24 (€30.48) 8pm, 24 hours notice, unavailable
  Sunday & Monday
* Open 15 April until 30 September
* Credit Cards: Amex, Visa, Mastercard

Pyers & Marguerite O'Conor-Nash
Clonalis House,
Castlerea, Co. Roscommon.

Tel & fax: +353 907 20014

email:clonalis@iol.ie
http://ireland.iol.ie/~clonalis/

Directions:
On the west side of
Castlerea on the
N60.

Map Ref.
12

Coolclogher House

Coolclogher House is a handsome early Victorian house, set in a 60 acre walled estate in the suburbs of Killarney. The building is surrounded by mature gardens and dramatic parkland, with wonderful views of the surrounding mountains.

Mary Harnett and her husband Maurice restored the house to the highest standards, before opening to guests last year. Bedrooms are large and beautifully appointed, and the reception rooms are spacious, stylish and comfortable. These include the Victorian conservatory, built around a huge specimen camellia, more than 170 years old.

Completely secluded from the bustle of the town and in the centre of one of Ireland's most beautiful tourist locations, Coolclogher House is the best and most secluded accommodation currently available in Killarney, and is a perfect base for day trips to the Ring of Kerry, Dingle, Kenmare and Glengarriff. Local attractions include fishing, climbing, hill walking, cycling, horse riding and traditional music, and there are plenty of good restaurants to choose from nearby. The area is a golfer's paradise, convenient to the world famous courses at Killarney, Waterville and Ballybunion and is within walking distance of the 22,000 acre National Park which surrounds the famous lakes of Killarney.

* 4 bedrooms, all en-suite
* Price per person sharing £45–£65 (€57.15–€82.55)
  Single supplement: £30 (€38.10)
* Open 1 April to 30 October
* Children 8 years and upwards welcome
* Credit Cards: Visa, Mastercard

Mary & Maurice Harnett
Mill Road,
Killarney, Co. Kerry.

Tel: +353 64 35996
Fax: +353 64 30933

Directions:
Take 3rd turning off the N71 (Muckross Road) as you leave Killarney town. Gates on right after one mile.

Map Ref.
13

Creagh House

A Classical Regency townhouse with stately reception rooms, spacious bedrooms and large bathrooms, beside the Awbeg River on the edge of Doneraile town. Creagh House is an important listed building, with historical and literary connections with Thackeray, Elizabeth Bowen, Canon Sheehan and Daniel O'Connell.

Here you can enjoy a timeless country house atmosphere, although there are traditional pubs and other amenities within easy walking distance. Supper is available (with advance notice) and there is a wide range of restaurants within a short drive.

The historic town of Doneraile is an ideal base for visiting scenic, cultural, historic and sporting sites in Munster. Doneraile Court, Mallow Racecourse and Blarney are nearby. Killarney and Cashel are within an hour's drive, as are Cork and Shannon Airports.

---

* Three double en-suite rooms
* B&B: £55 (€69.85). Single supplement: £10 (€12.70)
* Supper: £10 (€12.70) 8–10pm. Book by noon
* Open February to November
* Credit Cards: Amex, Visa, Mastercard
* Private Car parking

Michael O'Sullivan & Laura O'Mahony
Creagh House,
Main Street,
Doneraile, Co. Cork.

Tel: +353 22 24433
Fax: +353 22 24715

email:creaghhouse@eircom.net
www.creaghhouse.ie

Directions:
Take N20 (Limerick Road) from Mallow. At New Twopothouse (4 miles) turn right for Doneraile (4 miles).

Delphi Lodge

Delphi Lodge, Ireland's most famous fishing lodge, was for many years the sporting playground of the Marquis of Sligo. A large, comfortable 1830s country house, with great atmosphere, it is set in a deep valley of unparalleled beauty. The spectacular mountain location has inspired many writers over the years and Delphi was recently described by the New York Times as "an inviolable wilderness preserve" and by the Financial Times as "an estate of fabulous beauty".

The famous Delphi Fishery offers private fly-fishing for wild salmon and sea trout on a delightful little river and lake system.

Though fishing is a primary pastime, Delphi is also popular with hill walkers, artists, golfers and horsemen and, being very remote, it offers real peace and relaxation to all guests. On wet days a billiard room, an eclectic library and a fine wine list help to pass the time. Guests normally eat together at a vast oak table and the atmosphere is that of a friendly house party.

---

* 12 rooms all en-suite
* B&B: £40–£60 (€50.80–€76.20). Single supplement: 50%
       Lakeview supplement: £20.00 (€25.40)
* Dinner: £27 (€34.29) 8pm, 6 hours notice
* Fishing prices: £30 to £80 per day (Book well in advance).
* Whole Lodge bookings possible October to January
* Open all year (except Xmas and New Year)
* Not recommended for young children. Dogs not allowed in house
* Five charming cottages also available on the Estate
* Credit Cards: Visa, Mastercard

Peter & Jane Mantle
Delphi Lodge,
Leenane, Co. Galway.

Tel: +353 95 42222 Fax: +353 95 42296

email:info@delphilodge.ie
www.delphilodge.ie

Directions:
Turn north off N59
4km east of Leenane.
Continue towards
Louisburgh for 9km.
House is in woods on
the left, 1km after
adventure centre.

Emlaghmore Lodge

Emlaghmore was built in 1862 as a small fishing lodge on the edge of the Roundstone Bog, 150 square miles of moorland and lakes which are a Special Area of Conservation for otters, raptors and unusual plants.

It has its own river running through the garden with fly fishing for Sea Trout, Brown Trout and the occasional Salmon, yet is only a few hundred yards from the Atlantic and its rocky islands and sandy beaches.

Emlaghmore is comfortably furnished in accordance with its age, and has belonged to the Tinne family for over 75 years. Situated halfway between the picturesque fishing village of Roundstone and the 18-hole links golf course at Ballyconneely, it is an ideal place to relax and enjoy Connemara.

There are good pubs and restaurants in the area, and local activities include sailing, sea fishing, riding, hill walking, windsurfing, bird watching and painting.

---

* One twin and one double bedroom each with an en-suite bathroom
* One single bedroom with separate bathroom
* B&B: £30–£40 (€38.10–€50.80). Single supplement: £10.00 (€12.70)
* Dinner: £25 (€31.75) 8.30pm. Book in advance. Not available Saturday & Sunday
* Open April–September inclusive
* Wine Licence
* Credit Cards: Amex, Visa, Mastercard

Nicholas Tinne
Emlaghmore Lodge,
Ballyconneely,
Connemara, Co. Galway.

Tel: +353 95 23529
Fax: +353 95 23860

email:info@emlaghmore.com
www.emlaghmore.com

Directions:
Callow bridge is on the coast road, six miles from Roundstone and $2^1/_2$ miles from Ballyconneely.
100 yards on the Roundstone side of the bridge, take the road inland. 2nd gate on right.

Map Ref.
16

Enniscoe House

Enniscoe House is listed as a heritage house and has passed to Susan Kellett by inheritance. Its elegant plasterwork and elliptical staircase are renowned. Family portraits, antique furniture, good food & wine, all contribute to the pleasant, relaxed atmosphere.

The house is on the shores of Lough Conn, with attractive views of the lake across the parkland. The old walled garden is being restored and another garden produces organically grown vegetables. Outbuildings contain a small agricultural museum and a genealogy centre that researches names and families of Mayo origin. The fishery manager can make all arrangements for trout and salmon fishing in the area; tuition is a speciality. Three golf courses and riding stables are within easy reach. The house is a good base for touring Mayo and Sligo.

---

* Six rooms, all with private bathrooms
* B&B: £54–£66 (€68.58–€83.82). Single supplement: £10 (€12.70)
* Children under 12: 50%
* Children under 2, sharing: free
* Dinner: £28 (€35.56) book by 4.00pm
* Dogs welcome by arrangement
* Open April 1 to October 14
* Credit Cards: Amex, Visa, Mastercard

Susan Kellett
Enniscoe House,
Castlehill (near Crossmolina),
Ballina, Co. Mayo.

Tel: +353 96 31112
Fax: +353 96 31773

email:mail@enniscoe.com
www.enniscoe.com

Directions:
4.5 km south of Crossmolina on the road to Pontoon & Castlebar and 20km from Ballina.

Map Ref.
17

Farran House

Originally built in the mid 18th century, Farran House was remodelled in 1863 in the elegant Italianate style you see today. It is located in the rolling hills of the lee valley in 12 acres of mature beech woodland and rhododendron gardens, overlooking the medieval castle and abbey of Kilcrea.

The house has been carefully restored and retains its original character and charm. All four bedrooms have large bathrooms and beautiful views over the surrounding countryside. In addition to the antique furnishings, you will also find a grand piano in the drawing room and the billiard room has a full-sized table.

Farran House is a perfect base for exploring counties Cork and Kerry. It is 9 miles from Blarney, 38 miles from Killarney and 10 miles from Cork City and airport. Golf (six 18-hole courses within 20 miles), fishing (Rivers Lee and Bandon) and riding stables are all within easy reach.

* Four bedrooms, all with private bathroom
* B&B: £49–£55 (€62.23–€69.85). Single supplement: £15 (€19.05)
* Dinner £25 (€31.75) 24 hours notice, unavailable
  Sunday & Monday
* Advance bookings only
* Special rates available for longer stays
* Open 1 April to 31 October
* Groups by arrangement at other times
* House also available for self-catering
* Children accepted
* Credit cards: Amex, Visa, Mastercard

Patricia Wiese & John Kehely
Farran House,
Farran,
Co. Cork.

Tel: +353 21 733 1215
Fax: +353 21 733 1450

email:info@farranhouse.com
www.farranhouse.com

Directions:
Farran House is 10 miles west of Cork, on the N22. From Ballincollig 2nd right after Dan Sheahans, then right again up hill. First gate on left.

Map Ref.
18

Fermoyle Lodge

Fermoyle, a fine Victorian sporting lodge, is tucked away in one of the wildest and most remote parts of Connemara. From its wilderness setting there are spectacular views over Fermoyle Lake to the distant Twelve Pins.

It is an ideal location for sporting pursuits, with salmon and sea trout fishing (fly only) on the doorstep and several golf courses within easy reach. A 15 minute drive enables guests to reach the Connemara coast, with its many sandy beaches, or the ferry to the magical Aran Islands. Fermoyle is just 29 miles from Galway City and its airport and 2½ hours from Shannon.

* Four bedrooms all with private bathrooms
* Mews Two double bedrooms, both with private bathrooms
* B&B: £45–£55 (€57.15–€69.85). Single supplement: £20 (€25.40)
* Dinner: £25 (€31.75) 7.30pm, 24 hours notice required
* Open 30 March until 28 October
* Group bookings welcome all year round
* Unsuitable for young children and dogs
* French spoken
* Credit cards: Visa, Mastercard

Nicola Stronach
Fermoyle Lodge,
Costello,
Co. Galway.

Tel: +353 91 786111
Fax: +353 91 786154
email:fermoylelodge@eircom.net
www.fermoylelodge.com

Directions:
From Galway take N59 towards Clifden. In Oughterard, turn left just before bridge & follow signs for Costello. Lodge is 11 miles from Oughterard on right.

Frewin

Frewin is an important, unaltered Victorian house, in mature wooded grounds, on the outskirts of historic Ramelton. Formerly the rectory, the house has been painstakingly restored and authentically furnished by Thomas and Regina. They and their family offer their guests a warm welcome in an atmosphere of comfort and relaxation. Supper is available (with advance notice).

Ramelton is an unspoiled Heritage Town at the mouth of the River Lennon, on the western shore of Lough Swilly, and boasts a number of fine examples of the architecture of the 17th century and Georgian periods. It is an ideal base for walking or touring Donegal's wild mountainous countryside and spectacular coastline, with fine beaches, golf courses, tennis, fishing, leisure centres and restaurants in the area.

* 4 bedrooms, 3 en-suite
* B&B: £35–£45 (€44.45–€57.15). Single supplement: £10 (€12.70)
* Open all year
* Not suitable for under 12's
* Group bookings welcome
* Entire house available on request
* No facilities for dogs
* Smoking restricted to Sitting Room and Library
* Dinner: £20 (€25.40) by prior arrangement
* Credit cards: Visa, Mastercard

Thomas & Regina Coyle,
Frewin,
Ramelton,
Co. Donegal.
Tel & Fax: +353 74 51246
email: Flaxmill@indigo.ie
www.accommodationdonegal.net

Directions:
Take the R245 from Letterkenny and travel 8 miles. Turn right on approaching Ramelton: gates on right after 300 yards.

Map Ref.
20

The Hidden
Ireland
2 0 0 1

17

15

32

16

19

Kr

12

Gal

ATLANTIC
OCEAN

11

Shannon

Lin

22

Farranfore

3

21

13

Lakes of
Killarney

18

7

Baldon

Glendalough House

Glendalough is a charming Victorian country house, built in 1840, with magnificent views of Caragh Lake and the McGillycuddy Reeks. Furnished with antiques and old paintings, the house has interesting gardens with mature trees and many rare shrubs.

Gillies can be arranged for trout and salmon fishing. Woodland walks, horse riding, golf on a number of championship courses and hill climbing are all available nearby.

Delicious dinners by candlelight make use of local produce such as wild salmon and succulent mountain lamb.

Glendalough is a house for all seasons and an excellent base from which to tour the Dingle Peninsula and the Ring of Kerry, with their many ancient ruins and historic sites.

* 3 double rooms, 2 twins, all with private bathrooms
* Mews – two double rooms en suite
* B&B: £50 (€63.50). Single supplement: £15 (€19.05)
* Dinner: £26 (€33.02) Mon to Sat 8pm, 24 hours notice
* Unsuitable for children
* No dogs in house
* Open 1 March until 31 October. Closed August 10, 11, 12
* Credit Cards: Visa, Mastercard, Amex

Mrs Josephine Roder-Bradshaw
Glendalough House,
Caragh Lake,
Co. Kerry.

Tel & Fax: +353 66 9769156

email:kerryweb@eircom.net
www.kerryweb.ie

Directions:
From Killorglin take Ring of Kerry road (N70) towards Glenbeigh for 5km. Turn left at sign for Glendalough & Caragh Lake and continue to end of road.

Map Ref.
21

Glenlohane

With furniture and memorabilia that depict the family's 250 years of residence, "tranquility" and "comfort" are two words that immediately come to mind in describing Glenlohane. In a parkland setting, overlooking terraced lawns, the rolling fields and trees of a 300-acre farm surround the house.

Guests are ideally located for daily sightseeing trips across the entire scenic Southwest. With notice, arrangements can be made locally for riding, salmon and trout fishing on the River Blackwater, and for fox hunting with the Duhallow Hunt. For golfers, there are 17 golf courses within an hour's drive.

The house is well suited for "home away from home" bookings for families or small groups of 6-10 people, who would like the privacy of the entire house with full service.

Desmond and Melanie offer their guests a comfortable and relaxed stay in a gracious setting that remains essentially unchanged after more than two centuries.

* Five bedrooms with private bath and/or shower
* B&B: £55–£65 (€69.85–€82.55). Single supplement: £10 (€12.70)
* Dinner: £25 (€31.75) 8pm, 24 hours notice, unavailable Sunday
* Dogs by arrangement
* Suitable for children over 12
* No smoking indoors
* The entire house may be reserved by a single party
* Open all year
* Credit Cards: Amex, Visa, Mastercard.

Desmond & Melanie Sharp Bolster
Glenlohane,
Kanturk,
Co. Cork.

Tel: +353 29 50014
Fax: +353 29 51100

email: info@glenlohane.com
www.glenlohane.com

Directions:
From Kanturk, R576 towards Mallow. Bear left on R580 towards Buttevant. First right towards Ballyclough. First residential entrance on left after 2.25km. No sign.

Glenview House

Glenview house is a family run Georgian Home (1780). Once part of the Fota Estate, it is set in 20 acres of garden, surrounded by forestry and woodland walks. Incorporating fine architectural and decorative features recovered from a Georgian terrace in Fitzwilliam St. Dublin, the house offers a special blend of tranquillity and civilisation. An ideal escape from the bustle of everyday life.

Glenview offers good wine, excellent food and a relaxed country lifestyle.

Despite its seclusion, Glenview is only 3 miles from Midleton and 13 miles from Cork. Kinsale, Blarney, Jameson Heritage Centre, Fota Wildlife Park, Cobh, Lismore, plus lots of outstanding countryside and coastline and 16 golf courses, are all within easy reach.

---

* 3 Double rooms and 1 Twin Bedroom all with private bathrooms
* 1 fully w/c accessible)
* B&B: £40 (€50.80)
* Single supplement: £8 (€10.16)
* Dinner: £25 (€31.75) 8pm, 12 hours notice
* Open all year
* Credit cards: Amex, Visa, Mastercard.

Ken and Beth Sherrard
Glenview House,
Midleton, Co. Cork.

Tel: +353 21 4631680
Fax: +353 21 4634680

email:glenviewhouse@esatclear.ie
www.dragnet-systems.ie/dira/glenview

Directions:
From Midleton take L35 towards Fermoy for 4km to a forested area. Take first left and then immediately right up hill. Glenview is the first entrance gate on left.

Map Ref.
23

Hilton Park

If you are looking for a calm, beautiful place where you can relax and take life gently and eat imaginatively cooked, homegrown food among friendly people, this is it. Hilton has been the Madden family home since 1734 and the furnishings, portraits and memorabilia have the harmony of long association.

All rooms have stunning views over the 500 acre wooded park or the restored gardens and lake. Many say the dining room is their favourite in the country.

Hilton is not a place to rush through and is an ideal centre from which to visit Castle Coole, Florence Court, Crom, Marble Arch Caves and all of Lough Erne; Ulster and the Midlands are at your feet. The Maddens have a special itinerary of little known, local antiquities. For stay-at-homes there are books, golf, fishing, boating and bicycles for hire.

---

* Six rooms, all with private bathrooms
* B&B: £64–£75 (€81.28–€95.25). Single supplement £20 (€25.40)
* Dinner: £27.50 (€34.92) 24 hours notice
* No children under 8
* No dogs in house
* Smoking restricted
* Open 1 April to 30 September
* Open off-season by arrangement for groups and parties
* Closed Sundays and Mondays
* Advance booking essential
* Credit Cards: Visa, Mastercard.

Johnny & Lucy Madden
Hilton Park,
Clones, Co. Monaghan.

Tel: +353 47 56007
Fax: +353 47 56033

email:jm@hiltonpark.ie
www.hiltonpark.ie

Directions:
From Dublin take N3 to Cavan, follow the by-pass (signed Ballyshannon), turn rt. for Ballyhaise (2nd junction). Go through Ballyhaise and Scotshouse, gates on left after Golf Club. From Clones gates on right, 3 miles out on Scotshouse road.

Map Ref.
24

Kilmokea

Kilmokea, a Georgian house built in 1794, has been lovingly restored and stands in seven acres of heritage gardens on the banks of the River Barrow. The bedrooms in this former rectory have been lavishly decorated; one has a four-poster and another a Bateau Lit. All overlook the gardens, which include a formal walled garden, full of rare and tender species from all over the world, and a woodland garden, with many walkways and exciting displays of exotic plants.

Private trout fishing and aromatherapy treatments are available for guests, as is a whole range of home-grown produce.

Twelve golf courses are within easy reach and horse-riding, deep-sea fishing and water sports can all be arranged. The nearest ports and airports are Rosslare Harbour (45 mins), Waterford Airport (25 mins) and Cork Airport (110 mins). Dublin is two hours away.

---

* 6 bedrooms, 5 en-suite, 1 with private bathroom
* B&B: £45–£80 (€57.15–€101.60). Single supplement: £15 (€19.05)
* Dinner: £28 (€35.56) 8pm, book by noon
* Open 1 February to 4 November
* Credit cards: Visa, Mastercard, Laser

Mark and Emma Hewlett
Kilmokea, Great Island,
Campile, Co. Wexford.

Tel: +353 51 388109
Fax: +353 51 388776

email:kilmokea@indigo.ie
www.kilmokea.com

Directions:
From New Ross take the R733 signposted Campile & JFK Arboretum and follow signs to Kilmokea Gardens. Turn right to Great Island, cross causeway, Kilmokea at top of incline.

Map Ref.
25

Lismacue House

C

Lismacue was purchased in 1705 by William Baker, a direct ancestor of Kate Nicholson, the current owner. The present house was completed in 1813 to the design of architect William Robertson. It is a classically proportioned Irish country house set in 200 acres and approached by one of the most impressive lime tree avenues in Ireland, planted c.1760.

The drawing room and library still carry the original wallpaper. The bedrooms offer wonderful views of the surrounding countryside. Available locally are golf (five courses within 30 minutes), horse riding, hill walking and trout fishing on the estate's own river. Foxhunting is organised from October to March.

* Three rooms with private bath. Two other rooms
* B&B: £45–£55 (€57.15–€69.85). Single supplement: £11 (€13.97)
* Dinner: £26 (€33.02) book by noon, unavailable Sunday
* Suitable for children
* No dogs allowed
* Open 17 March to 31 October
* Groups welcome at other times
* House available to rent on weekly basis
* Credit Cards: Amex, Visa, Mastercard
* French spoken

Jim & Kate Nicholson
Lismacue House,
Bansha, Co. Tipperary.

Tel: +353 62 54106
Fax: +353 62 54126

email: info@lismacue.com
www.lismacue.com

Directions:
From Tipperary,
take N24 through
Bansha towards
Cahir. The entrance
is just outside
Bansha on the left.

A warm welcome is assured at Lorum. Set beneath Mt. Leinster in the tranquil Barrow Valley, the Rectory, built in 1863 of cut granite, is filled with pleasant conversation and the exciting aroma of freshly baked bread. This family run home has built a reputation for its warmth of welcome and imaginative home cooking – using home or locally produced ingredients wherever possible.

Whatever their requirements, guests at Lorum are spoiled for choice. Carlow, Kilkenny, Wexford, Waterford, Kildare and Wicklow are all within easy reach (and even a day-return to Dublin by rail is possible). For those in search of peace and tranquillity, the gardens at Kilfane, Woodstock and Altamont are ideal. There is golf at Mt. Juliet, Mt. Wolsley and Borris and fishing, walking or cycling alongside the Barrow River if you need a little exertion. Or you can play croquet, wander in the garden or wonder who painted the sheep?

You will enjoy your stay at Lorum with Bobbie and Don.

* Five en-suite bedrooms
* B&B: £37.50–£40 (€47.62–€50.80). Single supplement: £15 (€19.05)
* Dinner: £27.50 (€34.92) book by noon
* Open 3 January until 21 December
* Credit Cards: Amex, Visa, Mastercard

Don & Bobbie Smith
Lorum Old Rectory,
Kilgreaney,
Bagenalstown, Co. Carlow.

Tel: +353 503 75282
Fax: +353 503 75455

email:bobbie@lorum.com
www.lorum.com

Directions:
Midway between
Bagenalstown and
Borris (7km from
both) on the R705.

Martinstown House

Originally part of the extensive estates of the Dukes of Leinster, Martinstown was completed by the Burrowes family between 1832–40 in the charming Strawberry Hill gothic style as a cottage orné. Many interesting people have stayed here, and today's visitors enjoy old-fashioned hospitality but with modern-day comforts. The house is beautifully decorated and has an informal elegance with a most welcoming atmosphere.

Outside there are wonderful trees, a well-maintained walled garden with a hard tennis court, an old icehouse, cattle, sheep, two donkeys and proper free-range hens.

Nearby racecourses include the Curragh, Naas and Punchestown. The National Stud and Japanese Gardens are 4 miles away. For golfers there are several challenging courses within 30 minutes. Dublin is 32 miles and the Wicklow Mountains are reached well within the hour, as is Dublin Airport.

* 4 double rooms with private bathrooms
* B&B £70 (€88.90) for single nights stay
* £60 (€76.20) for 2–3 nights stay
* £55 (€69.85) for 4 or more nights
* Single supplement: £10 (€12.70)
* Dinner £30 (€38.10) 24 hours notice, unavailable Sunday
* Unsuitable for small children. No pets please.
* Open 8 January until 10 December
* French spoken
* Credit Cards: Amex, Visa, Mastercard

Mrs. Thomas Long
Martinstown House,
The Curragh, Co. Kildare.

Tel: +353 45 441269
Fax: +353 45 441208

www.hidden-ireland.com/martinstown

Directions:
Kilcullen exit off M9
then N78 towards Athy.
Sign at 1st crossroads.
Or off N7 in Kildare
pass entrance to
National Stud &
Japanese Gardens, fork
right to Bush Pub &
follow signs.

Map Ref.
28

Mobarnane House

Hidden away in the Golden Vale of Tipperary, Mobarnane is a special secret waiting to be discovered. Recently lovingly restored by Richard and Sandra Craik-White, the house provides a high standard of accommodation where you are looked after with flair, and in great comfort.

At the heart of Mobarnane is a Tower House, built in the early 1600's, with Georgian additions from 1730 and 1820 when the house was completely remodelled and given its present classical front. It is set in 60 acres of pasture with woodland, gardens and an ornamental lake. Mobarnane makes a perfect base for exploring Tipperary: the area is renowned for arts and crafts, golf courses, mountain scenery, castles and cathedrals, and of course for the breeding and training of world-class race horses.

Richard trained at The Grange and guests will find his and Sandra's careful attention to detail provides a totally relaxing experience. Dinner is eaten at one large table.

* 4 bedrooms, including 2 suites with sitting rooms, all with en-suite bathrooms
* B&B £55–£65 (€69.85–€82.55). Single supplement: £10 (€12.70)
* Reduction of 20% for third and subsequent nights
* Dinner £27.50 (€34.92) 24 hours notice
* Open all year. Winter/Christmas house parties welcome
* Unsuitable for young children or those who find stairs difficult
* Dogs and Horses by arrangement
* Smoking restricted
* Credit Cards: Visa, Mastercard

Richard and Sandra Craik-White
Mobarnane House,
Fethard, Co. Tipperary.

Tel & Fax: +353 52 31962

email:info@mobarnanehouse.com
www.mobarnanehouse.com

Directions:
From Fethard, take the Cashel road. After 3.5 miles turn right, signed Ballinure and Thurles. House is 1.5 miles on the left.

Mornington

C

Tranquillity and warm hospitality are the essence of Mornington, home to the O'Hara's since 1858. Set in an unexplored corner of Westmeath, with its charming landscape of rolling hills, ancient forests and sparkling lakes, Mornington is truly part of the real hidden Ireland, away from the tourist hordes, yet just 60 miles from Dublin.

The original manor was built in 1710 and extended in 1896. It is now a gracious family home with a reputation for delicious meals prepared in the fine tradition of the Irish country house. Anne is a member of Euro-toques, the international fraternity of serious chefs.

Excellent golf, fishing and equestrian facilities can be arranged. The neolithic sites at Newgrange and Loughcrew and the early Christian sites at Fore and Clonmacnoise are all within easy reach, as are the gardens and castles of Ballinlough, Tullynally and Butterstream.

* 4 double & 1 single room, all with private bathrooms
* B&B: £40 (€50.80). Single supplement: £7.50 (€9.52)
* Dinner: £25 (€31.75) 8pm, book by 2pm
* 3-day half-board rate: £179 (€227.33)
* Children by arrangement. No dogs in house.
* Open: March 31 to October 31
* Open for groups at weekends in November and St. Patricks weekend.
* Credit Cards: Amex, Visa, Mastercard

Warwick & Anne O'Hara
Mornington,
Multyfarnham,
Co. Westmeath.

Tel: +353 44 72191
Fax: +353 44 72338

e-mail:info@mornington.ie
www.mornington.ie

Directions:
From N4/Mullingar bypass take R394 for 8km to Crookedwood. Left at Wood Pub, then 2km to first junction. Go right, house is 1km on right.

Map Ref.
30

Number 31

Hidden behind a high wall right in the heart of Georgian Dublin is where you will find Number 31, an oasis of tranquillity and greenery just a few minutes from St. Stephen's Green. The Museum, National Art Gallery, Trinity College and the main shopping district are all a short walk away.

Number 31 is the former home of Ireland's leading architect Sam Stephenson. Guests are encouraged to come back and feel at home at any time of the day. A great variety of rooms are spread over the two buildings, the coach and a fine Georgian townhouse overlooking Fitzwilliam Place. Vast breakfasts, including lots of home made goodies, are served in the dining room and the roof conservatory in the coach house.

---

* Eighteen rooms, all with private bathrooms
* B&B: £45–£75 (€57.15–€95.25). Single supplement £15 (€19.95)
* Dinner not served but many restaurants within walking distance
* Children over 10 years of age welcome. No pets please.
* Open all year
* Credit cards: Amex, Visa, Mastercard

Noel & Deirdre Comer,
Number 31,
31, Leeson Close, Dublin 2.

Tel: +353 1 6765011
Fax: +353 1 6762929

email:number31@iol.ie
www.number31.ie

Directions:
From St. Stephen's Green, go past Shelbourne Hotel up Merrion Row, turn right at Pembroke St. Turn left onto Leeson St. Leeson Close is next left.

Map Ref.
31

The Quay House

The Quay House is Clifden's oldest building, dating from c.1820. It was originally the harbourmaster's house but later became a Franciscan monastery, then a convent and finally a hotel owned by the Pye family. It is now run as a town house by the Foyle family, whose forebears have been entertaining guests in Connemara for nearly a century. The Quay House stands right on the harbour, just 7 minutes walk from the town centre. All rooms are individually furnished with some good antiques and original paintings; several have working fireplaces and all but two overlook the harbour. All have large bathrooms with tubs and showers and there are also two ground floor rooms for wheelchair users.

The owners are always on hand for advice on local activities i.e. fishing, horse riding, golfing, hiking etc. There are several excellent restaurants and pubs within walking distance.

---

* 14 bedrooms all en-suite
* B&B: £45–£50 (€57.15–€63.50). Single supplement: £15 (€19.05)
* Open mid-Mar. to mid-Nov. (other months by arrangement)
* Children accepted
* Credit cards: Visa, Mastercard

Paddy & Julia Foyle
The Quay House,
Clifden, Co. Galway

Tel: +353 95 21369 Fax: +353 95 21608

email:info@thequayhouse.com
www.thequayhouse.com

Directions:
3 minutes from
town centre on the
harbour.

Map Ref.
32

Red House

Red House, a delightful Georgian house, was the home of the politician Chichester Fortescue (Lord Carlingford) and the Countess Waldegrave, a famous hostess. Guests included lions of Victorian society such as Edward Lear.

The beautiful landscape of Louth has plenty to offer, especially to sportsmen. Racing, foxhunting, shooting and golf are all available locally. Guests have access to Slane Castle to fish for salmon and trout on the River Boyne. Other attractions are Newgrange, the round tower and crosses at Monasterboice, the ruins of Mellifont and the magnificent scenery of the Cooley peninsula.

The house has its own floodlit tennis court, indoor heated swimming pool and sauna (summer months) The elegant rooms overlook parkland which has been well maintained for 200 years.

* One double room with bath & shower
* Two twin/double rooms with adjacent bath or shower
* B&B: £35–£45 (€44.45–€57.15). Single supplement £10 (€12.70)
* Dinner: please enquire when booking
* Open all year except mid December to mid January.
* Credit Cards: Amex, Visa, Mastercard

Linda Connolly
Red House,
Ardee,
Co. Louth.

Tel & Fax: +353 41 6853523

Directions:
Just North of Ardee on N52.

email:redhouse@eircom.net
http://homepage.eircom.net/~redhouse

Map Ref.
33

Roundwood House

Roundwood is a wonderful, small, 18th century Palladian house close to the magnificent and unspoilt Slieve Bloom Mountains in the heart of Ireland. It is 5km from the main Dublin-Limerick road and just 90 minutes from the centre of Dublin or from Shannon Airport. The house is surrounded by fine woods of chestnut, beech and lime.

The dining room, drawing room and study contain a large collection of books, paintings and antiques. For children there are games to play, animals to feed, woods to explore and the company of other children. Sportsmen will find riding and three golf courses available locally. There is abundant wildlife in the neighbouring woods and moors. Birr Castle is just 30km away and Kilkenny is 48km.

* Ten bedrooms, all with private bathrooms
* B&B: £47.25 (€60.01). Single supplement: £11.81 (€14.99)
* Dinner: £27.55 (€34.99) book before noon
* No Sunday lunch
* Open 2 February 2001 until 6 January 2002
* Children accepted
* Credit Cards: Amex, Visa, Mastercard, Diners Club, Laser

Frank & Rosemarie Kennan
Roundwood House,
Mountrath,
Co. Laois.

Tel: +353 502 32120
Fax: +353 502 32711

email:roundwood@eircom.net
www.hidden-ireland.com/roundwood

Directions:
From Mountrath 5km NW on R440 in direction of Slieve Bloom mountains. Follow signs.

Map Ref.
34

Simmonstown House

Simmonstown House is a late Victorian town house in a quiet cul-de-sac in Ballsbridge, Dublin's most elegant district. The house was extensively restored in 1988 and refurnished in period style, retaining all the original features. Guests enjoy all modern comforts but in a graceful setting, complete with antiques and paintings, which have been collected over the years. Simmonstown has a deserved reputation for its delicious breakfasts, served in the elegant dining room.

The house is within walking distance of the city centre and is very close to the main bus and DART rail services. Top quality restaurants are but five minutes' walk away.

* Four bedrooms, all with private shower rooms
* B&B: £50–£70 (€63.50–€88.90)
* Single supplement: £10 (€12.70). Children under 12: 50%
* Children under 2, sharing: free
* Dinner not served but many restaurants within walking distance
* Open 10 January until 20 December
* Credit cards: Amex, Visa, Mastercard

James and Finola Curry
Simmonstown House,
Sydenham Road, Ballsbridge,
Dublin 4.

Tel: +353 1 6607260 Fax: +353 1 6607341

email:info@simmonstownhouse.com
www.simmonstownhouse.com

Directions:
Sydenham Road is a cul-de-sac off Merrion Road and directly opposite the Royal Dublin Society; just minutes from the American Embassy.

Map Ref.
35

Streeve Hill

Streeve Hill, built by Conolly McCausland in 1730, stands within the demesne of Drenagh. It has a Palladian facade of rose brick and enjoys fine views over parkland to the distant Sperrin Mountains. Recent renovations have combined contemporary comforts with 18th century charm.

The gardens of Drenagh are nearby with their fine Italian terraces and enchanting Moon Garden.

Streeve Hill is renowned for its gourmet dinners and irresistible breakfasts. It is ideally placed for visits to Downhill, the Giant's Causeway and Donegal. There are several golf courses nearby, including Castlerock and Royal Portrush. Also available are tennis, riding, shooting and fishing.

* Three bedrooms, all with private bathrooms
* B&B: Stg£40–stg£45. Single supplement: Stg£10
* 10% discount for stays of two nights.
* Three nights plus: 15% discount
* Dinner Stg£30.00 Available June, July and August (except Sunday and Monday) 24 hrs notice required. Dinner at other times by prior arrangement
* Children welcome. No dogs allowed.
* Open 1 February until 30 October
* Credit Cards: Amex, Visa, Mastercard

Peter & June Welsh
Streeve Hill, Limavady,
Co. Londonderry, BT49 0HP.
Tel: +44 28 777 66563
Fax: +44 28 777 68285

www.hidden-ireland.com/streeve

Directions:
From Limavady take B201 (but B119 on signpost!) signed for Castlerock, for half mile then follow estate wall on right. 200 yards past gate lodge turn right at end of wall.

Map Ref.
36

Temple House

Temple House is a Georgian mansion set in an estate of 1000 acres, overlooking a 13th century lakeside castle of the Knights Templar. The Percevals have lived here since 1665. The present house was refurbished in 1864 and retains its old atmosphere, furnishings and some canopied beds.

Deb is a member of Eurotoques and uses produce from the walled garden and the estate which runs sheep and Kerry cattle. There are terraced gardens and miles of woodland walks. Guests may also explore the lake in a rowing boat or fish for pike. Within easy reach are beautiful beaches, archaeological sites, riding schools, trout lakes and golf courses. Traditional music and dancing sessions are often held nearby.

* 6 bedrooms, 5 en-suite
* B&B: £42–£45 (€53.34–€57.15). Single supplement: £10 (€12.70)
* Dinner: £20 (€25.40) book by noon
* Children's high tea: 6.30pm
* Open April 1–Nov 30
* Children accepted. No dogs in house
* **Sandy is very allergic to scented products. Please avoid all perfumes, after shave and aerosol cans.**
* Credit Cards: Amex, Visa, Mastercard

Sandy & Deb Perceval
Temple House,
Ballymote, Co. Sligo.

Tel: +353 71 83329
Fax: +353 71 83808

email: guests@templehouse.ie
www.templehouse.ie

Directions:
Signposted from Ballymote and on the N17, 24km south of Sligo.

Map Ref.
37

Tyrella House

C

Hidden away under the Mourne Mountains and sheltered from the sea breezes by tall beech woods, Tyrella's grasslands sweep down to a private sandy beach. After a day of fresh sea air, Tyrella is a wonderful place to relax and enjoy delicious dinners, perhaps of home grown lamb and vegetables from the garden.

Guests can ride over one of Tyrella's cross country courses or gallop on the sandy beach that stretches for miles in either direction. For garden and architecture lovers there are the National Trust houses at Mountstewart, Castleward and Rowallane. Fishing can be arranged and guests can play golf at Newcastle. Tyrella has its own polo ground: lessons or chukkas are available.

* Three bedrooms, all with private bathrooms
* B&B: Stg£40. Single supplement: Stg£10
* Dinner: Stg£22 (24 hours notice)
* Kennels & stables available
* Advance booking essential
* Open 1 February until 12 December
* Credit Cards: Visa, Amex

David & Sally Corbett
Tyrella House,
Downpatrick,
Co. Down.
Tel & Fax: +44 28 44851422

email:tyrella.corbett@virgin.net
www.hidden-ireland.com/tyrella

Directions:
Tyrella's Gate Lod
with blue gate
7km from Clo
the Clough/
Road.

Map Ref.
38

Whitfield Court

Whitfield Court is a Georgian Palladian house with intriguing architecture, including three distinctly different external elevations and a splendid dividing staircase. Surrounded by woods and countryside, Whitfield stands between an Upper and a Lower Park containing several ancient specimen trees. Your hostess, Maria-Ines is a Ballymaloe-trained Chef and her husband, Hugh, is a Senior Polo Coach.

Two polo fields and 20 ponies offer visitors the opportunity to play or just spectate from May to September. There are 12 golf courses within an hour's drive and many places to visit, including Kilkenny Castle. Just 10 minutes from Waterford Crystal's showroom, Whitfield is also close to Waterford Airport (15 mins), Cork Airport (90 mins), and Rosslare Harbour (60 mins); Dublin is 2 hours away.

* Four bedrooms, all with private bathrooms
* B&B: £50–£60 (€63.50–€76.20). Single supplement: £10 (€12.70)
* Dinner £29.90 (€37.97) 8 pm, 24 hours notice
* Open 15 April until 30 September
* No children or dogs
* Spanish spoken
* Credit cards: Visa, Mastercard

Hugh & Maria Ines Dawnay
itfield Court,
ford,

51 384216
71 384539

nay@tinet.ie
nd.com/whitfield

Directions:
On N25 from Waterford towards Cork, 6 miles from Waterford Quay, entrance on left with black gates.

Map Ref.
39

The ideal gift

The Hidden Ireland Vouchers make
the ideal present for anniversaries,
birthdays, weddings or indeed
any special occasion.

Vouchers are available in
denominations of £25, £50 and
£100 and may be used as payment
or part payment for a stay in any
Hidden Ireland house.
We will be delighted to send your
gift cheques to the
recipient with your own
personal message enclosed.

For further details please contact:

The Hidden Ireland

P.O. Box 31, Westport, Co. Mayo, Ireland.
Telephone: +353-1- 662-7166
Fax: +353-1- 662-7144
Toll free in USA: - 1800-688-0299
email: info@hidden-ireland.com
www.hidden-ireland.com

$\mathcal{E}$UROPE
of $\mathcal{T}$RADITIONS

www.europetraditions.com

'Europe of Traditions' is a consortium of five organisations, offering a personal style of hospitality in homes of character. All are interested in preserving and helping their guests to enjoy the heritage and culture of their country and their region, be this reflected in the architecture, or food and wine.

ESPAÑA ESPACIO ATLÁNTICO
FRANCE ESPACE ATLANTIQUE
IRELAND ATLANTIC AREA
PORTUGAL ESPAÇO ATLÂNTICO
U.K. ATLANTIC AREA

The Hidden Ireland is a member of Europe of Traditions which receives financial assistance from the Interrege IIC programme.

PORTUGAL
Solares de Portugal – Turihab
Praça da República, 4990 Ponte de Lima - Portugal
Tel: (+351) 258 742827   Fax: (+351) 258 741444
info@turihab.pt
www.turihab.pt

IRELAND
The Hidden Ireland
P.O. Box 31, Westport, Co. Mayo, Ireland
Tel:(+353 1) 6627166   Fax:(+353 1) 6627144
Email: info@hidden-ireland.com
http://www.hidden-ireland.com

FRANCE
Cháteau Accueil
Le Prieuré Saint-Michel
61120 - Crouttes - France
Tel: (+33) 2 33 391515   Fax: (+33) 2 33 361516
chateau-accueil@acs.fr
www.chateau-accueil.com

UNITED KINGDOM
Wolsey Lodges
9 Market Place, Hadleigh, Ipswich, Suffolk IP7 5DL,
United Kingdom
Tel: (+44) 1473 822058   Fax: (+44) 1473 827444
wolsey@wolseylo.demon.co.uk www.wolsey-lodges.co.uk

NETHERLAND
Erfgoed Logies
Rijksstraatweg 18
NL 9752 AD Haren, Netherland
Tel: (+31) 50 5350202   Fax: (+31) 50 5350203
info@ergoedlogies.nl
www.erfgoedlogies.nl

PORTUGAL
Europe Traditionae Consortium
Praça da República
4990 Ponte deLima - PORTUGAL
Tel: (+351) 258 742827   Fax: (+351) 258 741444
info@europetraditions.com
www.europetraditions.com

HOUSES, CASTLES & GARDENS OF IRELAND

There is no better way of experiencing the heritage of Ireland than visiting the many houses, castles and gardens open to the public.

The contents of all of these properties are rich in interest. Some have splendid plasterwork or art or furniture collections. Many are still owned and lived in by the descendants of those who originally built them.

There are examples of Irish homes from every period of our island`s past - from the Bronze Age to the Victorian era.

Gardens have been a priority with landowners. The moist maritime climate, tempered by the Gulf Stream, has encouraged the cultivation of an unrivalled range of plants from the Northern and Southern hemispheres and the creation of a rich and varied heritage of gardens, the earliest dating from the 17th century and the more recent created during the past 20 years, that are scarcely known. For a booklet contact:

Houses, Castles & Gardens of Ireland,
Lisdua, 16A Woodlands Park,
Blackrock, Co. Dublin, Ireland.
Tel/Fax: +353 (0) 2889114;
Mobile: +353 (0) 86 8300046
www.castlesireland.com
www.gardensireland.com
email: info@castlesireland.com
email: info@gardensireland.com

The Hidden Ireland Guide to Holiday Rentals

For more than 14 years The Hidden Ireland has provided visitors with an opportunity to experience our country from a different, more relaxed perspective. Since then our members have welcomed thousands of well-satisfied guests under their roofs. We have built up a loyal following, not just within Ireland, but from all over the world and our customers return each year to sample new houses and revisit old favourites. Many of you have become friends and valued supporters of our association and our unique product.

For the fourth consecutive year we offer self-catering accommodation in Hidden Ireland houses. These houses are all individual, reflecting their owners' personalities and interests. While they vary considerably, in size and price, there has been no compromise in quality. They are all in tip-top condition, with central heating, modern kitchens and bathrooms, and comfortable, stylish, well-furnished living areas and bedrooms.

Some houses are architecturally or historically important, or are attached to great gardens or estates. There are converted stables, mills and farm buildings, restored cottages and gate lodges, an entire county house, or just a self-contained wing. There are fishing lodges, offering the very best sport in the

country, which are equally attractive as a base for a week of golf or sightseeing. All are located in tranquil, beautiful, and interesting places such as woodland, parkland, moorland and mountainside, by lake, sea and river, and all offer unlimited access to their unspoilt environment. The owners, or their staff, are always on hand to offer help and advice, and will do their utmost to ensure that your stay is enjoyable.

A self-catering holiday with The Hidden Ireland is an exciting alternative to the experience of sharing our members' homes and is an ideal way to spend your holiday!

For a copy of
The 2001 Hidden Ireland Guide to Holiday Rentals
please contact us at

**Tel: +353 (0)1 662 7166 Fax: +353(0)1 662 7144
email: info@hidden-ireland.com
www.hidden-ireland.com
P.O. Box 31, Westport, Co. Mayo, Ireland**

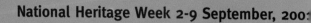

Open your eyes to Ireland's exciting heritage...

Yearly ticket available!

Explore national parks, gardens, historic houses, castles, monuments and nature reserves.

Dúchas offers a guide-information service and visitor facilities at over 65 sites throughout Ireland.

For further information:

email: heritagecard@ealga.ie
web: www.heritageireland.ie

Tel: +353 1 647 2461
Fax: +353 1 661 6764
Callsave: 1850 600 601 (within Ireland only)

An Roinn Ealaíon, Oidhreachta, Gaeltachta agus Oileán
Department of Arts, Heritage, Gaeltacht and the Islands

Dúchas
The Heritage Service

Notes

Directory

		Phone	Fax
1	Annesbrook	+353 41 9823293	+353 41 9823024
2	Ardnamona	+353 73 22650	+353 73 22819
3	Assolas	+353 29 50015	+353 29 50795
4	Ballinkeele House	+353 53 38105	+353 53 38468
5	Ballyowen House	+353 62 61265	–
6	Ballyvolane House	+353 25 36349	+353 25 36781
7	Bantry House	+353 27 50047	+353 27 50795
8	Blanchville House	+353 56 27197	+353 56 27636
9	Boltown House	+353 46 43605	+353 46 43036
10	Castle ffrench	+353 903 22288	+353 903 22003
11	Clifden House	+353 65 6837692	+353 65 6837692
12	Clonalis House	+353 907 20014	+353 907 20014
13	Coolclogher House	+353 64 35996	+353 64 30933
14	Creagh House	+353 22 24433	+353 22 24715
15	Delphi Lodge	+353 95 42222	+353 95 42296
16	Emlaghmore Lodge	+353 95 23529	+353 95 23860
17	Enniscoe House	+353 96 31112	+353 96 31773
18	Farran House	+353 21 7331215	+353 21 7331450
19	Fermoyle Lodge	+353 91 786111	+353 91 786154
20	Frewin	+353 74 51246	+353 74 51246
21	Glendalough House	+353 66 9769156	+353 66 9769156
22	Glenlohane	+353 29 50014	+353 29 51100
23	Glenview House	+353 21 4631680	+353 21 4634680
24	Hilton Park	+353 47 56007	+353 47 56033
25	Kilmokea	+353 51 388109	+353 51 388776
26	Lismacue House	+353 62 54106	+353 62 54126
27	Lorum Old Rectory	+353 503 75282	+353 503 75455
28	Martinstown House	+353 45 441269	+353 45 441208
29	Mobarnane House	+353 52 31962	+353 52 31962
30	Mornington	+353 44 72191	+353 44 72338
31	Number 31	+353 1 6765011	+353 1 6762929
32	The Quay House	+353 95 21369	+353 95 21608
33	Red House	+353 41 6853523	+353 41 6853523
34	Roundwood House	+353 502 32120	+353 502 32711
35	Simmonstown House	+353 1 6607260	+353 1 6607341
36	Streeve Hill	+44 28 777 66563	+44 28 777 68285
37	Temple House	+353 71 83329	+353 71 83808
38	Tyrella House	+44 28 44 851422	+44 28 44 851422
39	Whitfield Court	+353 51 384216	+353 51 384539

The Hidden Ireland Internet address

email: info@hidden-ireland.com
www.hidden-ireland.com

P.O. Box 31, Westport, Co. Mayo, Ireland